THE EVERYTHING WEDDING CHECKLIST

THE EVERYTHING WEDDING CHECKLIST

Janet Anastasio and
Michelle Bevilacqua
Illustrated by
Kimberly Young

BOB ADAMS, INC.
Holbrook, Massachusetts

Published by
Bob Adams, Inc.
260 Center Street, Holbrook, Massachusetts 02343

ISBN: 1-55850-278-5

Manufactured in the United States of America.

J   I   H   G   F   E   D   C   B   A

Library of Congress Cataloging-in-Publication Data
Anastasio, Janet.
        The everything wedding checklist : the gown, the guests, the
groom, and other things you shouldn't forget / Janet Anastasio
& Michelle Bevilacqua.
            p.   cm.
        Includes index.
        ISBN 1-55850-278-5 : $6.00
        1. Wedding etiquette. I. Bevilacqua, Michelle. II. Title.
        BJ2051.A535   1994
        395'.22—dc20   93-43272
                                                        CIP

*This book is available at quantity discounts for bulk purchases.
For more information, call 1-800-872-5627.*

TABLE OF CONTENTS

ACKNOWLEDGEMENTS

Sharon Capen Cook and Elizabeth Gale; Marie Luck Montillio of Bravo Montillio's; Susan Wright of Country Weddings; Christine Young, wedding consultant; Laura's Bridal Shop; Jeff at Merrill Graphics; Miller Studios; Flowers by Helen; Rev. Carol Atwood-Lyon; Father Dan Riley; Dawn Costello. Special thanks to Peter Gouck and Gigi Ranno for their patience and cooperation.

INTRODUCTION

Best wishes to you and your fiance' on your engagement. Now it's time for the exciting task of planning your wedding. Make no mistake, there'll be a lot to remember and a lot to do, but don't be daunted; The Everything Wedding Checklist can be a great help.

When should you start looking for your wedding gown? What time was that appointment with the baker? Who was that promising DJ your friends told you about? With this book you won't need to rack your brain for the answers to these and many more questions. Within these pages you'll not only find the answers you need, but a convenient place to keep track of names, appointments, and any other information you'll need to know while planning your wedding.

Whether it's picking a reception

site, finding a photographer, choosing flowers, or any of the other million things you'll need to do, this book can tell you when, where, and how to do them. The year-long planning calendar will put you on the right track and the subsequent checklists for each section will help you stay there. In addition, each chapter contains insights and advice on every aspect of your wedding, from finding a gown to picking a limousine.

In short, if you need to be informed about it or reminded to do it in order to plan your ultimate wedding, The Everything Wedding Checklist won't let you down.

SPECIAL ENGAGEMENTS

So, you're engaged. Now what?
After the dust settles from the whirlwind of excitement and celebrating with family and friends, there are some things you'll have to do to actually get married. Depending upon the type and size wedding you decide to have, you may have lots to do, or tons to do. In any event, the following schedule should give you a general idea of what has to be done, and when you should do it.

Six to twelve months before the wedding

- ☑ Announce engagement
- ☑ Decide on kind of wedding
- ☑ Decide time of day
- ☑ Decide location
- ☑ Set a date

- ☐ Set a budget
- ☑ Select bridal party
- ☑ Plan color scheme
- ☑ Select and order bridal gown
- ☑ Select and order headpiece
- ☑ Select and order shoes
- ☑ Select and order attendants' gowns
- ☑ Start honeymoon planning
- ☑ Go to bridal gift registry
- ☑ Start compiling the guest list
- ☑ Select caterer
- ☑ Select musicians
- ☑ Select florist
- ☑ Select photographer
- ☑ Start planning reception

☑ Reserve hall, hotel, etc., for reception
☑ Plan to attend premarital counseling at
   your church, if applicable
☐ Select and order wedding rings

Three months before the wedding

☑ Complete guest list
☑ Make doctor's
   appointments
☑ Plan to have
   mothers select
   attire
☑ Select and
   order invitations

NA ☐ Order personal
   stationery
☐ Start compiling
   trousseau
☑ Finalize reception arrangements (rent
   items now)
☑ Make reservations for honeymoon
☑ Confirm dress delivery
☑ Confirm time and date with florist
☑ Confirm time and date with caterer
☑ Confirm time and date with
   photographer
☑ Confirm time and date with musicians
☑ Confirm time and date with church

- ☐ Discuss transportation to ceremony and reception
- ☒ Order cake
- ☒ Select and order attire for groomsmen
- ☒ Schedule bridesmaids' dress and shoe fittings

Two months before the wedding

- ☒ Mail all invitations to allow time for R.S.V.P.s
- ☒ Arrange for appointment to get marriage license
- ☐ Finalize honeymoon arrangements

One month before the wedding

- ☒ Schedule bridal portrait
- ☐ Reserve accommodations for guests
- ☐ Begin to record gifts received and send ✓thank-you notes
- ☒ Plan rehearsal and rehearsal dinner
- ☐ Purchase gifts for bridal party
- ☒ Purchase gift for fiancé if gifts are being exchanged

necklace
bag
earrings
nylons
garter

☑ Schedule final fittings, including accessories and shoes

☑ Schedule appointments at beauty salon for attendants

❏ Schedule bridesmaids' luncheon or party

❏ Arrange for placement of guest book

❏ Obtain wedding props, e.g., pillow for ring bearer, candles, etc.

☑ Get marriage license

Two weeks before the wedding

N/A Mail bridal portrait with announcement to newspaper

❏ Finalize wedding day transportation

❏ Arrange to change name on license, Social Security card, etc.

❏ Confirm accommodations for guests

Prepare wedding announcements to be
mailed after the wedding

One week before the wedding

- ❑ Start packing for honeymoon
- ❑ Finalize number of guests with caterer
- ❑ Doublecheck all details with those
  providing professional services
  (photographer, videographer, florist,
  etc.)
- ❑ Plan seating arrangements
- ❑ Confirm desired pictures with
  photographer
- ❑ Style your hair with headpiece
- ❑ Practice applying cosmetics in proper
  light
- ❑ Arrange for one last fitting of all
  wedding attire

❑ Make sure rings are picked up and fit properly

☒ Confirm receipt of marriage license

❑ Rehearsal/rehearsal dinner (one or two days before wedding)

❑ Arrange to have the photographer and attendants arrive two hours before ceremony if there are to be pre-wedding pictures

❑ Arrange for music to start one half hour prior to ceremony

❑ Arrange to have the mother of the groom seated five minutes before ceremony

❑ Arrange to have the mother of the bride seated immediately before the processional

NA ❑ Arrange for the aisle runner to be rolled out by the ushers immediately before the processional

Your wedding day

❑ Try to relax and pamper yourself;

take a long bath, have a manicure, etc.
- ❏ Eat at least one small meal
- ❏ Have your hair and make-up done a few hours before ceremony
- ❏ Start dressing one to two hours before ceremony

Some general thoughts

Over the course of your planning, there are a few policies you should adopt to ensure that everything will go smoothly.

- ❏ Don't put off until tomorrow what you can do today. A cliché yes, but nevertheless applicable when it comes to planning a wedding. There will be plenty to do as your wedding grows near; don't make things worse for yourself by leaving everything to the last minute.

- ❏ Stick to your budget. If you have a well-thought-out budget, you'll make things a great deal easier on yourself. You won't go into the poorhouse over your wedding, and you won't

waste time pursuing options that you can't afford.

❏ Get everything in writing. There are a lot of crooked people and establishments in the wedding industry just waiting to take advantage of a starry-eyed couple. Don't let them ruin your wedding! Get every aspect of every purchase agreement in writing, so that if things don't come out to your satisfaction, you will have the proper recourse. Another way to keep from being a victim: get references from every single place you're even considering doing business with.

Your wedding party

As soon as you and your fiancé figure out who you want in your wedding party, get on out there and ask them. Giving people advance notice allows them the time to prepare for the extensive financial and time commitments involved in a wedding. It also gives you the breathing room to find replacements if your first choices can't accept.

Maid/matron of honor

Denise Whitaker

Phone 234-2822

Address

Bridesmaid

Phone

Address

Bridesmaid

_____

Phone_____

Address_____

_____

_____

Bridesmaid

_____

Phone_____

Address_____

_____

_____

Bridesmaid

_____

Phone_____

Address_____

_____

_____

Bridesmaid

_____

Phone_____

Address_____

_____

_____

Best man

_____John Hogsett_____

Phone_____

Address_____

_____

_____

Usher

_____

Phone_____

Address_____

_____

_____

Usher

_____

Phone_____

Address_____

_____

_____

Usher

_____

Phone_____

Address_____

_____

_____

Usher

_____

Phone_____

Address_____

_____

_____

Usher

_____

Phone_____

Address_____

_____

_____

Usher

_____

Phone_____

Address_____

_____

_____

Flower girl

_____ *Marley Vanbeean* _____

Phone_____

Address_____

_____

_____

Ring bearer

Eric Marshall

Phone_____

Address_____

_____

_____

Additional special attendants

Lauren Sauvelle

_____

_____

_____

_____

_____

_____

_____

_____

_____

_____

_____

MONEY, MONEY: THE BUDGET

A budget is the nasty little detail that has a very big influence on your wedding. Your budget (if you stick to it) will dictate the size and style of your wedding, as well as all the other little extras such as flowers, music, photography, video, transportation, and so on.

The first step towards figuring your budget is to sit down with everyone who may be contributing monetarily—your groom, your parents, his parents— and discuss the kind of wedding you'd like to have. Traditionally, the bride's family bears the brunt of the wedding expenses while the

GROOM'S BILLS

BRIDE'S BILLS

groom's picks up the tab for a few select things, but that is by no means set in stone anymore. These days it is not uncommon for the bride and groom to be responsible for the majority of the wedding expenses.

The traditional expenses of the bride's family:

- ☑ Bride's wedding gown and accessories
- ☑ Fee for ceremony location
- ☑ All reception costs (location rental, food, decorations, etc.)
- ☐ Flowers for ceremony and reception

- ☐ Music
- ☐ Photography (and video)
- ☐ Transportation (limosine rental, etc.)
- ☐ The groom's wedding ring
- ☐ Housing for bridesmaids
- ☐ Gifts for bridesmaids

The traditional expenses of the groom's family:

- ☐ The bride's wedding and engagement ring

- [ ] Marriage license
- [ ] Officiant's fee
- [ ] Housing for ushers
- [ ] Gifts for ushers
- [ ] Part of the bachelor party (with part of the expense being borne by the groom's friends)

If you have the funds available to finance the wedding of your dreams, consider yourself very lucky. But if you find yourself a few dollars short of your dream, don't despair! There are compromises and cuts you can make that will have little or no effect on you or your guests' enjoyment of the day. Have your invitations offset-printed instead of engraved; hold a buffet instead of a sitdown dinner; limit the use of elaborate flowers.

Ultimately, you'll need to prioritize the areas of your wedding so that you can spend money on what's most important to you, on the things you will carry with you from the wedding into your future. Be willing to drop the notion of serving steak at the reception in order to afford a good photographer. What makes your wedding memorable is the love and the people, not the elaborate extras.

NOTES

us- rings dress, bridesmaid dresses

mom - reception, flowers

Eric's mom -
rehearsal dinner
Bridal party flowers.

PICK OF THE LITTER: GIFT REGISTRY

Dave

Here's a way to have a say in the gifts you'll get. There's really no need to await each new package with horror, afraid it will contain some tacky atrocity. Why not fill out a gift registry at your favorite store—and await each present with breathless anticipation. The registry is a great thing for your guests, too; they won't have to wrack their brains thinking of an appropriate gift.

When making your wedding gift list. . .

❑ Shop with your groom so that you make choices together.

❑ Consider registering at two stores to give a wider price range to your guests.

❑ Discuss return policies with the bridal registrar.

❑ Ask for a preprinted

listing of gifts and household items the
store offers.

☑ List all pattern numbers and color choices.

☑ Inform your family and friends where
you're registered.

☑ Have the store suggest that guests send

their gifts to your home rather than bring
them to the reception.

☑ Inquire about a temporary insurance
policy that will cover the gifts while
they're being displayed in your home.

☐ Ask a reliable friend to transport any
gifts from the reception site to your home.

☒ Remember that if the wedding is
temporarily postponed, all gifts are kept.
If the wedding is canceled, all gifts must
be returned. Inform everyone of the
cancellation. (But there's no need to give
messy details.)

Donna

HELP, I NEED SOMEBODY: WEDDING CONSULTANTS

Most women today are busy juggling the duel demands of private life and a career. Add the daunting proposition of planning a wedding, and some women may find themselves getting a little, well, frenzied. Even if you have tons of spare time on your hands, you may still want someone to show you the ropes

WEDDING CONSULTANTS OLYMPICS

when it comes to planning your wedding. That's where wedding consultants come in. Whether you want someone to take you by the hand and do everything for you or you just need a little advice on a few key issues,

there's someone out there to help you. Of course, you'll have to pay a bit for the help, but the advice and services you will get (and the aggravation they will avoid) may be worth the dough.

INDEPENDENT CONSULTANTS

Weddings are the first and only business of independent consultants. If you wish, they will handle the whole wedding for you: flowers, food, photography, caterer, reception site, music, and everything else. The consultant can even serve as the master of ceremonies at the reception.

Costs for this kind of consultant can vary. Some charge a flat rate; others ask for anywhere from 10 to 20 percent of the total cost of the wedding. That can add up in a hurry, but to some brides, the experience and industry contacts of these consultants are worth the expense. (Note: Though these consultants will probably offer to coordinate your whole wedding, you should feel free to confine their role to the few areas you feel you need help in, if that's the way you'd prefer to go.)

STORE-AFFILIATED CONSULTANTS

These consultants are employed by bridal salons, reception sites, and other businesses that cater to weddings. Their knowledge is usually limited to a particular area of expertise—but it does have the advantage of being free, provided you give your business to the establishment that employs the consultant.

PICKING THE RIGHT PERSON

How should you go about picking the right consultant for you? As far as store-affiliated consultants go, you can't. You get whoever is employed by the store and available at the time you come in. You have no real choice— other than to shop somewhere else. With an independent consultant, on the other hand, you will want to select someone who listens to your needs and ideas, and who you feel is capable of handling the job. Ask friends, family, and coworkers for referrals. If they all come up empty, consult the local phone book and ask people in the industry, such as florists, photographers, and bridal shops. Below is a list of questions that should help you find the right independent consultant for you.

❑ How long has the consultant been in business? (Many years in business means lots of experience and contacts. It also means that a consultant is probably reputable, as he or she hasn't been run out of

SUPER CONSULTANTS

town by dissatisfied customers.)

❑ Is the consultant full-time or part-time?

❑ Can you get references from former customers?

❑ Is the consultant a full-service planner, or does his or her expertise lie only in certain areas?

❑ If the consultant isn't a full-service planner, what services does he or she handle?

❑ What organizations is the consultant affiliated with?

❑ Is the consultant scheduled to work with any other weddings that are on the same day as yours? (You don't want your consultant to be too busy with someone else to meet your needs.)

❑ How much (or how little) of the consultant's time will be devoted to your wedding?

❑ What is the cost? How is it computed? (Hourly? By percentage? A flat fee?)

❑ If the consultant works on a percentage basis, how is the final cost determined?

❑ Exactly what does the quoted fee include (or omit)?

ESTIMATE

Name _____

Address _____

_____

Appointment date _____

Services provided _____

_____

_____

_____

Fee estimate _____

NOTES

_____

_____

_____

_____

_____

_____

_____

_____

"I NOW PRONOUCE YOU . . .": THE CEREMONY

Squaring away the details of your ceremony should be one of your first and highest priorities. If you don't know the time

and date of the ceremony, then you certainly can't do much reception planning.

As for the kind of ceremony you'll have, you should first decide whether it's going to be religiously-based or a civil act.

(Note: Marriage requirements and specific ceremony rites will vary from religion to religion. If you are interested in having a religious ceremony, consult with your officiant as soon as possible to learn what restrictions and guidelines will apply.) If you decide on a civil ceremony, don't feel tied to the old stereotype of a quick, drab exchange of "I do's" in a judge's chambers. With the exception of a religious site, you can have your civil ceremony anywhere you wish—and make it as beautiful and spirited as you've ever dreamed.

It's advisable to set a ceremony date six to twelve months before you want the wedding to occur, paricularly if you want a date during the peak time between April and October. Competition for ceremony sites in those months can be pretty fierce, so you're more likely to get the day and time you want if you start looking early. If you don't plan on having that long an engagement, the best rule to follow is to arrange the date as soon as you possibly can.

When you meet with your ceremony officiant to discuss a wedding date, make sure to have a list of questions ready for him or her to answer. You should also find out what you will be required to do. Here is a list of potential questions you might ask:

- Are there any restrictions placed on your ability to marry?
- What is the procedure for an interfaith marriage?
- Are there any papers to be filled out, bans to be posted?
- Are there any premarital counseling requirements? If so, what are they?
- What does the ceremony consist of?
- Will you be permitted to write your own vows?
- What kind of services does the facility provide (music, reception area)?
- What fees are required for marrying in the facility? What are the costs?
- What do the fees include?
- Can you include family members and close friends in the ceremony as readers, candle lighters, singers, and such?

❑ Will the facility provide any decorations? Carpeting? Aisle runner? Ribbon?

❑ Are there any restrictions as to the kind of music you can have at the ceremony?

❑ What are the rules regarding photography and video recording?

❑ Will you be dealing with a coordinator for the ceremony site over the course of planning the ceremony, or speaking directly with the officiant?

❑ Do they have facilities for the bridal party to wait and freshen up in while they wait for the ceremony to begin?

❑ Are there any other weddings that day?

❑ What about custodial services after the wedding?

❑ Is there room to have a receiving line at the back of the facility? What about outside, in a courtyard or garden?

❑ What is the parking situation?

Ceremony

Site _____

Address _____

_____

Officiant name _____

Phone number _____

Additional meetings/premarital counseling sessions

Place _____

Date _____

Time _____

Place _____

Date _____

Time _____

Place _____

Date _____

Time _____

DA DUM DE DUM: CEREMONY MUSIC

Before you begin to pick out music for your wedding ceremony, be sure to check with the officiant of your house of worship for guidelines. There always seem to be new policies on what selections are appropriate in a religious setting; what was forbidden last year may be accepted next month. It's a good idea to find out what you can and can't use before you get your heart set on something.

You should also. . .

- ☐ Meet with the musical director from your house of worship to discuss appropriate selections.
- ☐ Discuss fees for the organist and any

additional musicians that may be provided.

❑ Begin to choose the selection for each distinct part of the ceremony at least two months before the wedding.

THE PRELUDE

The prelude sets the mood. . . and provides a little listening enjoyment for your guests while they await your arrival.

Selections

_____

_____

_____

_____

At the conclusion of the prelude, the mother of the bride is seated. This is a good time to feature a song with a vocalist.

Selection

_____

_____

_____

∾ 34 ∾

THE PROCESSIONAL

The processional is played as the wedding party makes its way down the aisle. When the bride begins her march down, something selected especially for her is played. (An alternative, however, is for the bride to walk down the aisle to the same tune as the rest of the party, played at a different tempo.)

Selections

_____

_____

_____

THE CEREMONY

During the ceremony itself, you may wish to hear songs that have a special

meaning for you and your groom. If nothing comes to mind, ask your officiant for ideas. He or she will probably be able to suggest dozens of wonderful songs that can add meaning to what's taking place.

Selections

_____

_____

_____

THE RECESSIONAL

The recessional is played at the conclusion of the ceremony, as the members of the wedding party make their way back down the aisle. It's usually an upbeat and joyful selection, one that echoes the feelings of the newly joined couple.

Selections

_____

_____

_____

A MOVING EXPERIENCE: YOUR WEDDING TRANSPORTATION

Almost anything that moves can be used to transport you and your wedding party to the wedding. Although limousines are still the most popular mode of wedding transportation, don't overlook the possibility of dropping down to the ceremony in a hot-air ballon, or floating up on a sailboat. There are dozens of options. If the cost of the rental would fit into your budget, why not consider. . .

- ❏ A trolley car
- ❏ A horse and buggy
- ❏ A sleigh
- ❏ A plane
- ❏ A glider
- ❏ An antique car
- ❏ An Excaliber, a Rolls-Royce, a Bentley, or another make of luxury car
- ❏ A parade float
- ❏ A motorcycle
- ❏ A unicycle (well, maybe not—it

might be tough to manuver in the gown)

❑ A speedboat

. . . or anything else you can think of. Granted, some of these options aren't practical all year round, and others can be a logistical nightmare—not every ceremony site comes equipped with a landing strip—but the point is you do have choices beyond the traditional limousine.

Of course, whatever means of transportation you decide on for your wedding day should fit into your budget. To ensure that you'll be getting quality transportation for your money, you should ask certain questions of any company you rent transportation from.

(Note: the following list of questions is geared toward limousine rental, but it will give you an

idea of the kind of information you should get from any transportation supplier.)

❑ How long has the company been in business?

❑ Does the company have the proper license and insurance?

❑ Can you get references from former customers?

❑ Does the company own its vehicles? (Companies that don't own their own vehicles may have a hard time guaranteeing availibility. They are also less likely to be on top of any mechanical problems or other unforseen dilemmas.)

❑ Can you inspect the vehicles? (Check for cleanliness, dents, rust, and so on.)

❑ Does the company have the kind of vehicle you want? Will it be available on your wedding day?

❑ What are the rates? (Most limousine services charge by the hour.)

Unfortunately for you, the clock starts ticking the minute they leave their home base rather than when you start using the vehicle.)

❑ What is the company's cancellation policy?

❑ Is there a required minimum fee or number of rental hours?

❑ What is the policy on tipping? Is it included in the hourly rate, or should you account for it separately? (You won't want to tip your chauffeur at the end of the night if the gratuity is covered in the fee you paid. It's doubtful the service will be so spectacular that you'll want to pay twice!)

❑ How much of a deposit is required to reserve the vehicle(s) for your wedding? When is the final payment due?

❑ Will the company provide champagne? Ice? Glasses? A television? Will these items cost extra?

Before you give anyone

your business, make sure you can get a
written contract stipulating the date, time,
type of vehicle, services, and costs.

Company name

_____

Phone _____

Contact person _____

Phone _____

Type of vehicle _____

Number of people vehicle holds_____

Rental includes _____

_____

_____

_____

Rate (overtime also) _____

Cancellation policy _____

_____

Deposit required _____

Balance due _____

If you're not renting transportation, but, say, borrowing a nice luxury car from a family member or friend, make sure the car is tuned up, cleaned, and filled with gas. (You should offer to pay for the car wash and fill the tank with gas before and after the wedding.)

What about us?

You are also responsible for providing or arranging transportation for the members of your wedding party. You might also want to make sure your parents and the groom's parents won't be standing on the corner waiting for a bus to the ceremony. If your budget allows, consider renting an extra limousine or two to chauffeur them to and from the  ceremony and reception sites. Otherwise arrange for those with the nicest cars to transport the rest of the group. Make sure everyone is aware of who's taking whom, what time people will have to be ready, and where they may have to meet.

Wedding party transportation

Car/driver _____

Riders _____

_____

_____

_____

_____

Time _____

Meeting place _____

Car/driver _____

Riders _____

_____

_____

_____

_____

Time _____

Meeting place _____

TRANSPORTATION

Car/driver _____

Riders _____

_____

_____

_____

_____

Time _____

Meeting place _____

Car/driver _____

Riders _____

_____

_____

_____

_____

Time _____

Meeting place _____

The going-away car

The odds are good that your attendants will try to trash your going-away car. For safety's sake, make sure they don't obstruct the view or movement of the driver. Any writing should be applied with washable shoe polish.

If you're lucky, your budget will allow you to keep your limousine (or other rented transportation) until the end of the reception. As your attendants may not be too keen to trash a rented luxury car, you can whip over to your hotel (or to the airport) in style and not have to worry about cans clanging behind you all the way.

PRACTICE MAKES PERFECT: THE REHEARSAL & REHEARSAL PARTY

The purpose of the wedding rehearsal is to acquaint everyone in the wedding with the basics of the ceremony. Who (besides you and your groom) should attend? The officiant, every member of the wedding party, the father of the bride (to practice dragging her down the aisle, of course) any scripture readers and candle lighters, and any children taking part in the

ceremony. Invite the florist to discuss any final issues of flower placement. You might also want to arrange for any featured soloists or musicians to attend the rehearsal as well. Remember, this will be your only chance to iron out any last-minute details and resolve any remaining questions. Though it may not be enough to truly calm your nerves, by getting everything straight at the rehearsal

you can make sure that everything is ready and that all of the participants know what's expected of them.

The rehearsal is held at the ceremony site itself, usually on the night before the wedding. If that time is inconvenient for any of your key players, however, reschedule for another time, preferably during the week before the wedding. (If it's too far before the wedding, people may forget what they learned).

Rehearsal location _____

Address_____

Officiant_____

Phone_____

Date _____

Time _____

After your officiant meets the wedding party, he or she will give a quick overview of what will happen in the ceremony and who should be doing what. A quick practice runthrough of the ceremony is next, and that's it. If only the real ceremony could be that easy!

You might want to bring any essential items that you'll need for the wedding to the rehearsal. This way, you won't have to worry about carrying them with you in the limo ride to the ceremony.

❑ Wedding programs
❑ Unity candles
❑ Marriage license
❑ Fee for site
❑ Fee for officiant
❑ Practice bouquet
❑ Aisle runner

You might also bring along any last-minute information the wedding party will need, as well as any items that they may be in charge of bringing to the reception.

❑ Toasting goblets for reception
❑ Cake knife and server
❑ Guest book
❑ Seating cards for the reception
❑ Maps or written directions

❑ Wedding day transportation information

The majority of wedding rehearsals are merely a warm-up for the truly important event of the evening: the rehearsal party. The rehearsal party gives everyone involved in the wedding a chance to eat, drink, be merry, and hopefully relax and forget about the stresses of the big day to come.

Traditionally, the expense of the rehearsal party is borne by the groom's parents, but these days anyone who wishes may sponsor the party. A very informal affair, the rehearsal party usually takes place in a restaurant or a private home; a simple phone call is the usual means of inviting the guests.

And who should get an invitation?

- ❑ All members of the wedding party, along with their spouses or significant others
- ❑ The parents of the bride and groom
- ❑ The ceremony officiant, along with his or her spouse or significant other, if this is applicable
- ❑ Any special friends and family members
- ❑ Grandparents of the bride and groom
- ❑ Godparents of the bride and groom
- ❑ Out-of-town wedding guests

Of course, you can invite anyone else you want, but try to keep the party on the intimate side. Remember, the goal of this party is to let everyone relax and give you and your groom some additional time with loved ones who may only be in town for a few days. You'll have plenty of time to party with your other wedding guests on the big day.

A note on children at the rehearsal: their parents should be invited to the rehearsal party. But unless you are counting on a temper tantrum from an overtired child to be part of the reception entertainment, you should make sure the parents get the children home in time for them to get a good night's sleep.

Rehearsal Party Guest List

Name   Phone

_____

_____

_____

_____

_____

_____

_____

_____

_____

_____

_____

_____

_____

_____

_____

_____

_____

_____

Rehearsal party

Party location _____

Address_____

_____

Contact person _____

Phone_____

Time _____

FROM THE MOUNTAINS TO THE PRAIRIES... : RECEPTION SITES

The first thing you should do after securing a ceremony date and location is find a reception site. During peak wedding months (April-October) competition for sites is heavy; if you're marrying in this time frame, your best bet is to start looking at least a year in advance.

What are you looking for? You need a site that not only fits into your budget and can hold all your guests, but also presents an appearance and atmosphere you'd be happy with. If you'd like to get away from the traditional banquet hall reception, consider these alternatives:

- ❑ Castles, estates, or historic mansions
- ❑ Colleges and universities
- ❑ Plantations
- ❑ Concert halls
- ❑ Private or state parks
- ❑ Country inns
- ❑ Historic villages
- ❑ Historic hotels

- ❏ Luxury hotels
- ❏ Apple orchards
- ❏ Beach clubs
- ❏ Yachts, ships, boats
- ❏ Historic battleships
- ❏ Indian reservations or memorial sites
- ❏ Theaters
- ❏ Aquariums
- ❏ Observatories
- ❏ Museums
- ❏ Galleries
- ❏ Public or private gardens
- ❏ Night clubs
- ❏ Lighthouses
- ❏ Ranches/farmhouses
- ❏ Mountain resorts
- ❏ Waterfront restaurants
- ❏ Greenhouses

With any site you decide to visit, make note of architectural details, color schemes, and photography sites. Does the setting suit the mood you want to evoke? How well would this site fit into your dream vision of your wedding?

As easy as it is to get swept up in architecture and atmosphere, there are some practical matters you need to consider. If you find yourself seriously interested in a site, set up an appointment with the site coordinator as soon as possible. Get the following information.

Reception site:_____

Address: _____

_____

_____

Site coordinator: _____

Phone number: _____

Reception site:_____

Address: _____

_____

_____

Site coordinator: _____

Phone number: _____

During your meeting, make sure the coordinator can provide satisfactory answers to all of your questions.

❏ Is the site conveniently located?

❑ What size party can the site accommodate?

❑ What rooms are available?

❑ How long is the site available for? Is there a time minimum that must be met? Are there overtime charges if the reception runs late?

☑ Is there a dance floor? (What size?)

☑ Does the site have a catering service? Can you bring in your own caterer if you wish?

☑ Does the site provide tables, chairs, dinnerware, linens? What about decorations?

❑ Can the facility accommodate live music? Does it have the proper layout, wiring, and equipment?

❑ Does the site coordinator have any recommendations for setup and decorations? Can he or she recommend any florists, bands, disc jockeys, and such?

❑ Are there any restrictions regarding decorations, music or photography?

- ☐ Are there any photos of previous reception sites that you can see to get the overall feel of the place?
- ☐ What services come with the site? (Waiters, waitresses, bartenders, parking valets?)
- ☐ What is the standard server-to-guest ratio?
- ☐ What kind of reservation deposit is required?
- ☐ Will there be any other weddings at the site on the same day as yours?
- ☐ Is there a package plan? If so, what does it include?
- ☐ Are gratuities included in the quoted price?
- ☐ Is there any rental fee for table linens, plants?
- ☐ Does the price vary with the time of day?
- ☐ If it is an outdoor site, what alternate plans are there in case of inclement weather?
- ☐ Will the deposit be returned if you have to cancel?
- ☐ Does the

site have a
liquor license?
Liability
insurance?

☐ What is the
policy on open
bars? If you do
have an open
bar, are you responsible for providing the
liquor?

☐ Is there a corkage fee? (If you're
supplying your own liquor, some sites will
charge a corkage fee to cover the costs
of the staff opening bottles and pouring
drinks.)

☐ What are the drink prices at a cash bar?

☐ What types of beverages are available?

☐ Is there an added price for garnishes
for the bar?

☐ What is the layout of the tables? How
many people does each table seat?

☐ Is there enough parking? Is it free? If
there is valet parking, what is the policy
on rates and gratuities?

☐ Is there a coat-check room? Will there
be coatroom and restroom attendants? A
doorman? What are the charges?

☐ Is there a room that can be set aside for

picture taking?

❑ Are there changing rooms for the bride and groom?

❑ Who pays for any police or security that may be required?

❑ Can you see references?

Now you should have the facts and figures you need to determine whether or not this site meets your needs and your budget. A deposit (usually a hefty one) will reserve the site you want. But don't hand over any money until you get a written contract stipulating every term of your agreement. Signing a contract will also protect you from becoming a victim of escalating fees, which come into play when a couple reserves a site well in advance of the wedding date. Perhaps you've reserved the site in August for a wedding the following August. If you don't sign a contract specifying this year's prices, the site will try to charge you the new— higher—rates.

EAT, DRINK, AND (YOU HOPE) BE MERRY: PICKING THE RIGHT CATERER

If your reception site offers an in-house caterer that you find acceptable and that fits your budget, congratulations. Your work is already done! But if you have to find a caterer for yourself, bear in mind that prices and services vary greatly from caterer to caterer. Know what services you want in advance; don't waste your time interviewing candidates who can't provide what you need.

What services do you need? Let's

take it from the top.

Time of day of your reception:
- ☐ Morning
- ☐ Midday
- ☐ Midafternoon
- ☒ Early evening
- ☐ Evening

Style of reception:
- ☐ Breakfast/brunch, sitdown dinner
- ☐ Breakfast/brunch, buffet
- ☐ Brunch/luncheon, sitdown dinner
- ☐ Brunch/luncheon, buffet
- ☐ Buffet, hors d'oeuvres, cake and coffee
- ☐ Cocktail buffet
- ☐ Cocktails, dinner, and dance, sitdown
- ☒ Cocktails, dinner, and dance, buffet

(As you might imagine, the style is largely determined by the time of day you select.)

Here are some questions to ask potential caterers:

☒ What is the caterer's background and experience? (How many weddings has the firm handled? What was the largest? The smallest? Are references available?)

☒ Are package deals available? (In other words, can the caterer supply elements of the standard service—flowers and meals, say—and leave other elements—such as liquor—in your hands?)

☒ Is there an added charge for the staff's working time?

☒ Will you need to rent or borrow any serving pieces? (tables, chairs, equipment)

☐ Is the caterer in the restaurant business? (This is usually a good sign.)

☐ What color linens can the

caterer supply, if any?

☐ What kind of glassware does the caterer supply (wine/champagne stemware), if any?

☐ Are china and silverware part of the package?

☐ Can they supply the cake?

☐ Will the caterer try to charge you a "cake-cutting fee"? (If so, negotiate your way out of this, or find someone else. This charge is nothing but an excuse to pay people twice. Don't agree to do it.)

☐ Can you taste-test the meal options? (You might also want to ask to observe another wedding the firm is catering.)

☐ Are taxes and gratuities included in the

package?

❑ When do you have to supply the final guest count?

❑ Is there a list of client references you can contact?

❑ How will the fee be structured? Is it a flat rate, an hourly rate, or a package deal?

❑ How much of a deposit is required?

❑ Finally, ask the Better Business Bureau to supply you with information about any complaints that may have been filed against the firm. When working with a private caterer, make sure that all services and financial agreements are clearly understood.

Once you decide on a caterer, you will want to work together to establish your menu.

❑ Will the meal be served buffet-style? Sitdown-style? Russian-style (guests

 served food from platters brought to their tables)?

❑ What hors d'oeuvres will be served (if any)?

❑ What main course(s) will be served?

❑ What dessert(s) will be served?

If your reception site does not provide bar service, you are responsible for stocking the bar. Important note! If you will be operating the bar yourself, it must be an open bar (unless you have a liquor license). Selling liquor without a license is illegal.

Alcoholic beverages:

The following should be available at the bar.

Beer

Wine

Hard liquor

Champagne

Mixers

Lemons, limes, cherries, olives

Soda and other non-alcoholic beverages

Champagne punch

Non-alcoholic punch

Extras

Aside from the menu, what additional

services will the caterer be providing? Ask about. . .

- ❑ Waiters/waitresses
- ❑ Bartenders
- ❑ Valets

What equipment, if any, will you need to get from the caterer or rent yourself? Find out about. . .

- ❑ Tables and chairs
- ❑ Linens
- ❑ Dinnerware, glassware, silverware
- ❑ Coffee service

It's a deal!

Once everythings been decided on. . .

- ❑ Get every part of the agreement in writing (costs, services, date, time). The caterer should provide you with an

estimated cost per guest.

☐ Make sure the caterer is (or will be) well acquainted with the reception site and its facilities.

☐ Work up the final guest count and give it to the caterer.

☐ Ask the caterer whether the final cost per guest will differ from the initial estimate. If it will, ask by how much.

Caterer estimate

Name_____

Address_____

Phone_____

Contact person_____

Price per person_____

Total cost_____

NOTES

_____

_____

_____

_____

_____

PHOTOGRAPHY & VIDEOGRAPHY

Nothing but the best

You're spending a bundle on this wedding. Why not have some decent pictures to remember the day by? Of all the people and places you'll shell out money to over the course of your wedding, your photographer will be one of the most important. Imagine how heartbroken you'd be to find that the supposedly professional photographer you hired could only produce blurry, muddy photos—or worse yet, took all the photos with the lens cap on!

It may sound absurd, but such nightmares are not at all uncommon. Don't let yourself become another victim. Choose your photographer carefully; only sign on with

someone after you've seen his or her work and checked references.

Here is a list of questions that will help you choose the best man, woman, or studio for the job.

- ❏ How long has the photographer been in this business?
- ❏ Does the photographer specialize in weddings? (If he or she isn't a wedding expert, find someone who is.)
- ❏ Is this a full-time photographer? (Part-timers need not apply.)
- ❏ Can you see samples of previous work and speak to some former clients?
- ❏ What types of photo packages are offered?
- ❏ What is included in the standard package?
- ❏ What are the costs for additional photos?
- ❏ How many pictures does the photographer typically take at a wedding of this size?
- ❏ In addition to the base package fee,

will there be any additional hourly fees? Travel costs?

❑ Will you be charged by the hour?

❑ Does the photographer keep negatives? If so, for how long?

❑ May you purchase negatives if you wish?

❑ Will you be able to purchase extra photos in the future?

❑ Does the photographer use a variety of lighting techniques? A variety of backgrounds?

❑ Will the photographer take a mixture of formal and candid shots?

❑ Would the photographer be willing to incorporate your ideas into the shot list?

❑ Will the photographer provide a contract stipulating services, date, time, costs, and so on?

It's always wise to interview more than one photographer. That way , you can compare quality and prices to get the best person (and the best deal) for you.

Photographer

Name _____

Address _____

_____

Phone _____

Contact person _____

Number of proofs to be furnished _____

Total expenses (fee) _____

Click, click, click goes the shutter

Once you decide on a photographer, sit down with him or her to talk about the type and amount of photographs you'd like to see come out of your wedding. Remember, your photographer is there to meet your needs, but he or she won't be able to incorporate your ideas unless you communicate them.

The hit list

Make up a list of the posed pictures you'll want the photographer to take on your wedding day. Here are some suggestions.

- ❏ You and your groom
- ❏ You alone with your mother
- ❏ You alone with your father
- ❏ You with your mother and father
- ❏ You with the groom's parents
- ❏ The groom alone with his mother
- ❏ The groom alone with his father
- ❏ The groom with his mother and father
- ❏ The groom with your parents
- ❏ You and the groom with both sets of parents
- ❏ You with your attendants in a group
- ❏ The groom with his attendants in a group
- ❏ The whole wedding party
- ❏ You and the groom with grandparents, Godparents, and/or any favorite relatives

You're on candid camera!

You'll also want candid shots of the ceremony and reception.

Candid shots before the ceremony

- ❑ You and your attendants at your home before the ceremony
- ❑ Informal shots of you and your attendants at the back of the church or ceremony site
- ❑ Informal shots of you and your father before the ceremony
- ❑ You and your father arriving at the ceremony getting out of the car, and walking into the ceremony site
- ❑ You and your groom getting into the car
- ❑ You and the groom toasting one another in the car

Traditional ceremony "candids"

- ❏ Each attendant walking down the aisle, including flower girls, ringbearer, and pages
- ❏ Your mother coming down the aisle
- ❏ The groom's parents coming down the aisle
- ❏ You and your father coming down the aisle
- ❏ Your father leaving you at the altar
- ❏ Wedding party at the altar
- ❏ You and the groom exchanging vows and rings
- ❏ The lighting of candles and any other special ceremony features
- ❏ You and the groom kissing at the altar
- ❏ You and the groom leaving the ceremony

Reception candids:

- ❑ You and your groom arriving at the reception
  - ❑ Your first dance with the groom
  - ❑ You dancing with your father
  - ❑ The groom dancing with his mother
  - ❑ Cutting the cake and feeding it to each other

- ❑ Toasting each other
- ❑ Tossing the garter
- ❑ Tossing the bouquet
- ❑ You and the groom leaving the reception
- ❑ The "getaway" car
- ❑ Any other candid shots

Front-page news?

If you're planning to send a wedding

announcement

to the newspaper, be sure to inform your photographer so he or she can take a black-and-white portrait of the two of you as man and wife. Order an 5" X 7" glossy print to send to the paper.

TOTALLY UNHIDDEN VIDEO: TAPING YOUR WEDDING

With VCRs a standard feature in most American homes, it should come as no surprise that wedding videotapes are now as popular as traditional still photographs. How else are the bride and groom going to see and hear everything they were too excited or dazed to be aware of while it was actually happening?

Most couples consider their wedding videotape priceless, but that doesn't mean you have to shell out the family fortune to get a good one. As with still photography, you should be very careful about who you choose to trust with the valuable responsibility of videotaping your wedding. Ask the same types of questions and apply the same scrutiny that you did when choosing a photographer.

Here are some things you'll want to ask your videographer.

- ❏ How long has the person been doing this professionally?
- ❏ Can you see samples of the work and check references?
- ❏ Is the work guaranteed?
- ❏ Can you look at a work in progress in addition to a demo tape? (This way you'll know that the videographer is actually doing the work, not buying great demo tapes from someone else.)
- ❏ Is the equipment high-quality, including the editing and dubbing machines?
- ❏ Will the videographer be using a high-quality tape?
- ❏ How many cameras will be used? How big will the videographer's staff be?
- ❏ What special effects are available?

❏ Will you use wireless microphones during the ceremony so that the vows will be clearly heard on the tape?

❏ How is the fee computed? One flat rate? By the hour?

❏ Is a standard package deal offered? Is so, what is it?

❏ Are there ways to cut down on the total price?

❏ How much will it cost to have copies of the original made?

When viewing sample tapes, consider the following questions.

❏ Do the segments tell a story, giving a clear sense of the order in which the events took place?

❏ Does the tape capture the most important moments—such as you cutting the cake and throwing the garter?

❏ Is there steady use of the camera, clear sound, vibrant color and a nice sharp picture?

❑ How are the shots framed? What editing techniques are used?

❑ Does the tape move smoothly from one scene to the next—rather than lurching ahead unexpectedly?

Watch out!

It's usually not a wise idea to hire a family member or friend to be your videographer, even if they do have a shiny new camera. They may do adequate work, but odds are they still can't provide you with the same quality you'll get from a professional. (They probably won't have the necessary editing equipment, for one thing.). Friends and relatives are also more likely to get caught up in the action and forget that they're supposed to be filming it!

With all of the equipment and

technology available today, you should settle
for nothing less than a broadcast-quality
wedding video. Get the best deal for your
money, but don't choose someone cheap and
incompetent over someone who'll cost a little
more—but do a wonderful job.

Obviously, you'll want to interview
more than one videographer.

Videographer

Name _____

Address _____

_____

Phone _____

Contact person _____

Style _____

Total expenses (fee) _____

Finally, when you are sure you've
found the videographer you want, ask to sign
a contract with details such as date, location,
starting time, number of cameras, amount of
editing, name of camera person, names of
any assistants, end time and most important
the final cost.

Putting everything in place

Once you select a
videographer, take some

time to discuss the
type of video you
want. You will need to.

. .

❏ Find out whether
   your ceremony
   site puts any
   restrictions on
   camera
   placement.

❏ Take your videographer to the
   ceremony site so he or she can see the
   working conditions.

❏ Arrange for your videographer and
   photographer to meet (if they don't
   already know each other) so that they
   can get acquainted and coordinate
   their activities.

Name that format

There are various format options for
wedding videos. Here are a few you might
like to consider.

THE NOSTALGIC FORMAT

This type of video usually starts with vintage
photographs of you and your groom, perhaps
as children or young adults. From there, it
can show the two of you sharing your lives

together. The ceremony, reception, and (sometimes) shots of your honeymoon end this format. Because it takes a little more work to put together, this type of video can be expensive.

THE STRAIGHT SHOT FORMAT

This format uses only one camera, thus making it the least expensive video option offered. No editing is required, but the videographer can still add small touches, such as names and dates, to help spice up the film.

THE DOCUMENTARY FORMAT

As its title suggests, this format gives you a documentary style account of your wedding day. It usually starts with you and your groom getting ready, then proceeds to scenes of the ceremony and the reception; sometimes interviews with family and friends are added. The documentary format has become quite popular; the price will vary widely depending on the type of equipment used and the amount of editing needed.

The last word on video

Be sure to ask your videographer about any new technological advances in cameras, tapes, or editing that you might be able to take advantage of. Because technology develops so fast, there may be equipment available now that was unheard of last year. Currently, advances are being made with the new eight millimeter tape format. The eight millimeter tape provides a very high quality image and stands the test of time better than the standard VHS tape.

NOTES

_____

_____

_____

_____

_____

_____

_____

_____

_____

_____

_____

_____

MUSIC TO YOUR EARS

As soon as you've set a date for your wedding, you'll want to start thinking about hiring entertainment for your reception.

Most reception entertainment consists of a live band or a DJ, either of which should be reserved about three to six months in advance of your wedding date. Ask for suggestions from family and friends; if they come up empty, hit some area clubs and lounges and start listening. Before long, you'll understand why the good bands and DJs are always booked. You may have to dig a little to find someone you're happy with, but in the end, finding the right music option for you and your guests can make all the effort worthwhile.

What to look (and listen) for in a band:

❑ Do you like the group's sound? (Is it appropriate for your wedding?)

❑ How good is the band's sound system?

❑ Is their overall appearance and

demeanor positive? (Do band members look happy about what they're doing?)

❑ Do they have a wide repertoire of material? (Do they balance various styles well? Is there a good mix of fast and slow songs?)

❑ Would you trust the band leader to serve as master of ceremonies if need be? (Will he or she charge extra for this?)

You may decide that the best music option for your reception is a disk jockey. Hiring a DJ has several advantages: the selection of songs is greater, the logistical hassles are fewer, and the cost is less than a band's. However, many people consider a disk jockey to be a sign of a somewhat informal reception.

What to look (and listen) for in a DJ:

❑ Is the equipment and sound system of good quality?

❑ Does the DJ have a large selection of

records you and your guests will like?

❑ Does he or she mix different sounds and styles well? Is there a good mix of fast and slow songs?

❑ Would you trust him or her to serve as master of ceremonies, if need be? (Is there any additional fee for this?)

Once you find someone you like, it's time to talk terms:

❑ What are the costs?

❑ Are there any added fees not included in the quote?

❑ Will the DJ's/band's attire be appropriate for the reception?

❑ Is a special sound system or hook up required?

❑ What is the cancellation policy?

❑ What are the payment terms? (Ask about deposit and balance amounts.)

❑ What are the hourly overtime rates?

❑ If songs that are important to you are not currently in

the repertoire or play list, can they be added? Is there any additional charge for this?

And before you sign on the dotted line try to get the answers to these questions too. (You may want to visit the site with your band or DJ before making any formal commitment.)

- ❏ Can the reception site accommodate your band or DJ?
- ❏ Is there enough electrical power? Outlets? Space?
- ❏ How are the acoustics?

DJ/Band_____

Address_____

Phone_____

Contact person _____

Fee estimate _____

If you're like most couples, you will have special songs in mind that you want played at key points of the reception. List them here and you'll have a written record to share with your band or DJ.

LIST OF REQUESTS

Bride and groom's first dance:

_____

Bride and her father:

_____

Groom and his mother:

_____

Bride and groom's parents:

_____

Cake cutting:

_____

Bride tossing the bouquet:

_____

Groom throwing the garter:

_____

Bride and groom leaving the reception:

_____

Additional requests:

_____

_____

_____

_____

SCENT OF A WEDDING: YOUR WEDDING FLOWERS

With all this hectic wedding rush, wouldn't you like to sit back and take some time to smell the roses? Well, wait until you find a florist and choose your flower arrangements. Otherwise, there won't be any roses to smell!

Try to find a florist who comes with good recommendations from family or friends. Once you've selected a florist, make an appointment to meet with him or her to discuss your overall needs. (Be sure you have sample fabric of all the attendants' dresses on hand so you can match colors if you need to.)

Who and what will you be needing flowers for? This list below should give you a good idea.

FLOWERS FOR THE WOMEN

The Bride

☒ Bridal bouquet

Optional:

☒ A smaller bouquet, to throw at the bouquet toss

☒ Floral headdress

☒ Going-away corsage

To be delivered to

_____

_____

Time _____

Cost _____

BRIDAL ATTENDANTS

☒ Matron of honor

☒ Maid of honor

☒ Bridesmaids

☒ Flower girl

☒ Floral headdresses (if desired)

To be delivered to _____

_____

_____

Time _____

Cost _____

FLOWERS FOR THE MEN

The Groom and His Attendants

- ☑ Groom's boutonniere
- ☑ Best man's boutonniere
- ☒ Ushers' boutonniere
- ☑ Ringbearer's boutonniere

To be delivered to _____

_____

_____

Time _____

Cost _____

FLOWERS FOR THE FAMILY AND SPECIAL FRIENDS

☒ Bride's mother
☒ Groom's mother

Optional:
☐ Stepmother
☒ Grandmothers
☐ Mothers' roses
☐ Aunts, cousins, special friends

To be delivered to _____

_____

Time _____

Cost _____

FLOWERS FOR WEDDING HELPERS AND PARTICIPANTS (OPTIONAL)

☐ Bridal consultant

☐ Officiant

☐ Soloist

☒ Readers

☐ Instrumentalist

☒ Guest book attendant

☐ Gift attendant

☐ Others

To be delivered to _____

_____

_____

Time _____

Cost _____

Now that you've taken care of the people, it's time to start thinking about flowers for all of your wedding places.

CEREMONY SITE

- ❑ Arch/canopy
- ❑ Candelabra
- ❑ Altar floral spray
- ❑ Pews
- ❑ Aisles (runner)
- ❑ Other
- ❑ Kneeling cushion (for bride and groom)

To be delivered to _____

_____

_____

Time _____

Cost _____

REHEARSAL DINNER SITE

Centerpieces

To be delivered to _____

_____

_____

Date _____

Time _____

Cost _____

RECEPTION SITE

- ☐ Decorations, centerpieces for tables
- ☐ Main table
- ☐ Cake table
- ☐ Gift table
- ☐ Drapes, garland or greenery
- ☐ Flower petals for tossing
- ☐ Powder room
- ☐ Top of cake (if desired)
    - -Hanging plants
    - -Small trees

To be delivered to _____

_____

_____

Cost _____

    If you use a lot of floral arrangements at your wedding, put someone in charge of dispensing them after the reception. You may want to give the flowers to close friends or relatives, or perhaps to nursing homes or charitable organizations.

FLOWERS FOR AFTER THE WEDDING

    You might want to send thank-you flowers to mothers, friends, and relatives as a way of expressing your appreciation for all their help.

To be delivered to _____

_____

_____

Date and time _____

Cost _____

To be delivered to _____

_____

_____

Date and time _____

Cost _____

To be delivered to _____

_____

_____

Date and time_____

Cost_____

To be delivered to _____

_____

_____

Date and time_____

Cost _____

RECORD OF FLORIST

Florist Name _____

Phone_____

Address_____

_____

_____

Dates Ordered _____

NOTES

_____

_____

_____

_____

_____

_____

_____

_____

_____

YOU TAKE THE CAKE!

Long ago in medieval England, it was customary for each guest to bring a small cake or bun to a wedding. These days, the

marrying couple are responsible for providing their own cake. The wedding cakes of today are no simple affair: they may require a small army of bakers (and large chunks of time and money) to put together. Unless you can convince your guests they're in medieval England, here's what you're going to have to do:

- ☐ Begin searching for a bakery at least three months before the wedding.
- ☐ View the bakeries' sample books to find the right cake for you.
- ☐ Ask for taste tests of any style cake you're seriously considering.

- ❑ If the wedding cake is going to serve as dessert, tell the baker how many guests you expect.
- ❑ Find out how much of a deposit is required.
- ❑ Find out whether the deposit is refundable.
- ❑ Ask about any additional delivery or rental charges.
- ❑ Ask whether there will be a fee for having the baker set up the cake at the reception site.
- ❑ Ask whether the baker will supply a cake knife. (If not, you'll have to buy one.)
- ❑ If you want someone from the bakery to stay at the reception to help cut and serve the cake, find out the cost for this

service.

❑ Arrange when final payment for the
cake is due.

❑ Order the cake.

❑ Get a written contract stipulating type
of cake, cost, date of delivery, and any
other important specifications.

❑ Arrange for the baker to arrive at the
reception site before the guests to set
up the cake.

❑ Decide where the cake will be
displayed: on the head table or on a
table of its own.

A matter of taste...and design

Gone are the days of the plain white
wedding cake with plain white frosting. The
choices for cake flavors, frostings,
decorations, and garnishing are plentiful—
and tempting. Here
are just a few.

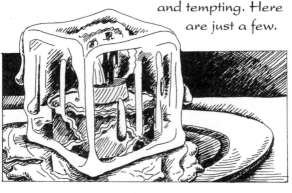

Cake flavors:

Chocolate
Double chocolate
Vanilla
White
Spice
Carrot cake
Cheese cake
Citron chiffon
Fruitcake
Chocolate hazelnut

Italian rum
Lemon
Orange
Raspberry
Strawberry
Chocolate mousse
Chocolate mocha
  spice
Banana

Fillings:

Lemon
Raspberry
Coffee
Strawberry

Vanilla
Butter cream
Custard

Sauces/toppings

Ice cream
Fresh fruit

Sweet fruit sauce
Hot chocolate sauce

And that's just the flavors! Your cake can be designed any number of ways, too— including

multiple tiers, stacked cakes, multiple sections, and even fountains! With so many options, coming to a final decision can be pretty hard. Here's a list of questions to ask your baker that might narrow things down a bit.

- [ ] What size cake should you have for the number of guests you're having?
- [ ] Can you have different flavors for different layers of the cake?
- [ ] What choices are available in cake flavors and frostings?
- [ ] Does the baker specialize in any flavor, style, or size?
- [ ] Is there a rental fee for tiers or separators?
- [ ] Can a small portion of the cake be prepared with brandy or another form of alcohol? (This will make it easier to eat a year from now if you decide to follow the tradition of freezing a small quantity of cake and sharing it with your husband on your first anniversary.)

Some weddings also feature a

groom's cake, traditionally a dark fruitcake packed into white boxes and given to the guests as a gift. Not everyone has a groom's cake these days. Couples who do often take a

lighthearted approach and have the cake decorated to resemble a hobby of the groom's. If your groom is a baseball fan, you might decide to have the cake shaped like a bat or a ball.

Usually the same baker makes both the wedding cake and the groom's cake.

❑ Pick a cake flavor and design (it doesn't have to be fruitcake any more!)
❑ Order the cake.
❑ Arrange for payment, delivery, and so on. Try to get a written contract just as you would with a wedding cake.

Bakery

Name _____

Address _____

Phone _____

Contact _____

Cake Flavors:

_____ Cost _____

_____ Cost _____

_____ Cost _____

Icing (frosting) _____

Number of tiers _____

Ornaments _____

Samples _____

_____

_____

_____

Notes _____

_____

_____

_____

DRESS TO KISS

Bridal attire

Shopping for your fairy-tale wedding gown can be a long and taxing process. On

top of the imposing proposition of finding the ideal gown, there is the added headache of dealing with bridal shop policies, politics, and potential disasters. Have you ever met a bride whose dress was not ready in time for her wedding? How about one who had the flimsy material of her gown rip as she was stepping out of the limousine? Even if you haven't, you can probably say with confidence that these "mishaps" are no one's idea of a good time.

How can you protect yourself? First, shop at only reputable places. If friends and family can't recommend a shop to you, check the pages of your local phone directory and visit area wedding expos. Once you find a place you're seriously considering doing business with, ask for references from former customers and check with the Better Business Bureau to verify that no complaints have been filed against the company.

You should begin shopping as soon as you become engaged. Ideally, you'll order your gown six to nine months before the wedding, as some gowns can take that long to arrive back from the manufacturer. With additional time required for alterations, you could still be cutting it a little close. If you don't have the luxury of that much time, there are shops that can turn around an order in three months, but they may have you pay for the express service, and you may not be able to order your first choice gown. If you decide to buy a discontinued or used gown, time is less of a problem; you just need to

concern yourself with getting the alterations completed.

Other gown shopping tips to be aware (and beware) of:

❏ Always talk to the manager of the shop. Find out how long the place has been in business. (You would hope that a disreputable establishment would not be around long.)

❏ Be careful of counterfit gowns. Some shops will tell you they carry brand name merchandise, when in fact the gowns are cheap imitations, sold to you at an "uncheap" price. (Call the dress manufacturer to verify that the shop is one of their authorized dealers.)

❏ Choose a delivery date for your gown that is several weeks before the wedding. (This should give you plenty of breathing room for alterations.)

❏ Make sure that the bridal shop doesn't try to get you to order a size that is much too big for you (i.e. a size 12 gown when you normally take a four)—that way you pay a small fortune for alterations.

☐ Don't allow the shop to use cloth measuring tapes. Over time, the cloth begins to stretch, often yielding incorrect measurements.

☐ Ask for verification of your order; call periodically to check on progress. (Sometimes the shops will hold your cash deposit for months before actually ordering your gown.)

☐ Get a written contract containing every aspect of your purchase agreement, including delivery date, cost of dress, cost of alterations, and any stipulations for refunds if the dress is not ready in time.

If you decide to forgo the bridal shop route and have your dress made by a private seamstress, you should still guard yourself against the typical pitfalls. In addition, you may have to order

your dress as much as a year in advance of your wedding, as that is how long it can take to make a gown from scratch.

BRIDAL SHOP

Name _____

Phone _____

Contact person _____

Gown description _____

_____

_____

_____

_____

Cost _____

ALTERATIONS/FITTINGS

Shop _____

Dates _____

_____

_____

Pick up date _____

Cost _____

THE PERFECT GOWN

What type of gown will you be looking for at the bridal shop or the seamstresses?

Most likely long and white, but after that basic decision is taken care of, the choices will appear virtually endless. As a guideline you might want to consider the degree of formality of your wedding, and, of course, your own personal taste.

Informal wedding:

- ❏ Formal, lacy suit or formal street-length gown
- ❏ Corsage or small bouquet
- ❏ No veil or train

Semi-formal wedding:

- ❏ Chapel veil and modest bouquet (with floor-length gown)
- ❏ Shorter fingertip veil or wide-brimmed hat and small bouquet (with tea-length or mid-calf-length gown)

Formal daytime wedding

- ❏ Traditional floor-length gown
- ❏ Fingertip veil or hat
- ❏ Chapel or sweep train
- ❏ Gloves

❑ Medium-sized bouquet

Formal evening wedding:

❑ Same as formal daytime except: Longer veil

Very formal wedding:

❑ Traditional floor-length gown (usually pure white or off-white) with cathedral train or extended cathedral train

❑ Long sleeves or long arm-covering gloves
❑ Full-length veil
❑ Elaborate headpiece
❑ Cascade bouquet

THE CROWNING TOUCH:
Headpieces and veils

Your headpiece and/or veil should complement your gown. There are plenty of options out there to choose from, but don't be shocked at the high pricetags, which border on the outrageous.

Although a headpiece/veil typically takes only eight to ten weeks to arrive after being ordered, you should consider placing your order even earlier. Having your headpiece or veil early will give you the luxury of a few trial runs with your hairdresser, to ensure you'll get the look you want.

Hairdresser

Shop_____

Contact person _____

Headpiece description _____

_____

_____

_____

_____

Cost _____

WEDDING PARTY ATTIRE

The bride has the privilege of selecting the final choice of fabric, color and style for the attendants dresses. Generally, the bridesmaids are dressed alike, but there is also the option of having the dresses differ in style, color, or both! Going this route makes it a lot easier to make every one happy, as a dress that looks great on one

woman can look like a potato sack on another. You can also have only the maid/matron of honor wear a different gown, to make her stand out more from the other attendants.

Try to keep in mind the following suggestions when shopping with your attendants.

❑ Check the formal dress section of a quality department store in your area before you go to a bridal salon. You may find appropriate dresses there that your attendants can wear again in the future—and at a cheaper price than salon dresses.

❑ The attendant's dresses should complement your gown.

❑ Ask the attendants opinions before deciding on a dress. Make sure the gown is one that looks good on everybody. (They are paying for this thing.)

❑ Try to keep the cost of the gown within reason.

❑ If all of your attendant's shoes have to be dyed the same color, it is best to have them dyed together, to ensure an exact color match.

THE FLOWER GIRL

You may want the flower girl's dress to match the attendant's dresses—or to be completely different. The dress may be short or floor length according to the style you want. If you have trouble finding something, a fancy party dress is a good—and inexpensive—choice.

THE GROOM AND HIS ATTENDANTS

Formal wear

These days, the groom and his attendants usually rent their formal wear. There are formal wear choices available to match the style demands of most weddings. All the men

need to do is tell the store attendant what their in the market for and they're in business.

Informal wedding:

- ❑ Business suit
- ❑ White dress shirt and tie
- ❑ Black shoes and dark socks

(For the winter, consider dark colors; in the summer, navy, white, and lighter colors are appropriate.)

Semi-formal wedding (daytime):

- ❑ Dark formal suit jacket (in summer, select a lighter shade)
- ❑ Dark trousers
- ❑ White dress shirt
- ❑ Cummerbund or vest
- ❑ Four-in-hand or bow tie
- ❑ Black shoes and dark socks

Semi-formal wedding (evening):

- ❑ Formal suit or dinner jacket with

matching trousers (preferably black)
- ❑ Cummerbund or vest
- ❑ Black bow tie
- ❑ White shirt
- ❑ Cufflinks and studs

Formal wedding (daytime):

- ❑ Cutaway or stroller jacket in gray or black
- ❑ Waistcoat (usually grey)
- ❑ Striped trousers
- ❑ White high-collared (wing-collared) shirt
- ❑ Striped tie
- ❑ Studs and cufflinks

Formal wedding (evening):

- ❑ Black dinner jacket and trousers
- ❑ Black bow tie
- ❑ White tuxedo shirt

- ❑ Waistcoat
- ❑ Cummerbund or vest
- ❑ Cufflinks

Very formal wedding (daytime):

- ❑ Cutaway coat (black or gray)
- ❑ Wing-collared shirt
- ❑ Ascot
- ❑ Striped trousers
- ❑ Cufflinks
- ❑ Gloves

Very formal wedding (evening):

- ❑ Black tailcoat
- ❑ Matching striped trousers trimmed with satin
- ❑ White bow tie
- ❑ White wing-collared shirt

- [ ] White waistcoat
- [ ] Patent leather shoes
- [ ] Studs and cufflinks
- [ ] Gloves

RINGBEARER/ TRAINBEARER

Most often the ringbearer and trainbearer are little boys, but they probably enjoy being dressed like the big guys. In most weddings, the ringbearer and trainbearers are dressed in the same basic outfit as the rest of the men (only in a much smaller size) or slight variation of the outfit featuring knickers or shorts.

The men should rent their formal wear one to three months before the wedding. Although a month is usually enough time to reserve the clothing in the "off season", it's better to be early and safe during peak wedding months (April-October). Obviously, the men should do business at a reputable shop, not one that will forget their order and rent out all of their tuxedos to prom-going high schoolers the morning of your wedding.

NOTES

_____

_____

_____

_____

_____

_____

_____

_____

_____

_____

_____

_____

_____

_____

_____

_____

_____

_____

YOU'RE CORDIALLY INVITED... : STATIONERY & INVITATIONS

While you can hire a private printer to create your wedding invitations, the most likely source for your invites is a local stationery or card store. There you'll find sample catalogs filled with dozens upon dozens of invitation styles, designs, and phrases. These stores are supplied by a few large manufacturers who seem to have the invitation market cornered these days. Because of their size and the volume they deal in, these manufacturers can offer more variety than a private printer—often at a cheaper price. The upside to smaller, private printers: they can do engraving (the most elegant form of invitation printing) and they can work in multiple ink colors.

Here are some basic questions you should ask yourself before

ordering your wedding invitations.

❏ What is the overall style and level of formality of the wedding? (Your invitations should reflect these things.)

❏ What do you want the invitation to say? How do you want the information worded?

❏ How do you want the words printed on the paper?

The answer to this last question is not as simple as whipping out the old Bic ballpoint and going to work. There are a number of more elegant options to choose from, depending upon your budget and your style preferences.

Engraving

As mentioned, engraving is the most elegant way of putting words on paper; unfortunately, it's also the most expensive. The paper is "stamped" from the back by metal plates the printer creates, which raise the letters up off of the paper as they are printed.

Thermography

This is the printing method used by most of the larger invitation printers. About half the price of engraving, thermography uses a method of heated ink printing that creates a look almost indistinguishable from engraving. Not surprisingly, it's quite popular.

Calligraphy

Calligraphy is that very fancy and intricate black script. Technically, calligraphy is done only by calligraphers who are trained in the art form. These people tend to charge a lot of money to perform their art, but don't rule out calligraphy yet. Some printers are now able to reproduce calligraphy by

means of a computer program, which is faster—and cheaper—than the human hand.

If your stationery store can't point you in the direction of a good calligrapher, check the local Yellow Pages; for computer generated calligraphy, your best bet is a small private printer.

Offset printing

Offset printing, also known as flat printing, is the most common form of printing. Though not as fancy as any of the other options, it is, as mentioned, the only form of printing that allows you to work with multiple ink colors. If you're interested in having your invitations done by the offset method, chances are you'll have to find a small private printer, as the larger ones tend to stick with thermography.

Hand-written invitations

If you are having fifty or fewer guests at your wedding, it is perfectly acceptable to

write out your invitations by hand. The only requirement here: whoever is going to do the writing should have legible handwriting.

In addition to these printing methods, there are hundreds of different styles and typeface to choose from. Take your time and pick a design you really like.

Note: Most invitation packages include response cards and reception cards, but check to make sure that you'll be getting them.

Stationery store (or printer)

Name _____

Address _____

_____

Phone _____

Contact person _____

Number of invitations _____

Delivery date _____

Price _____

Once you've picked out your invitations, sit down with your groom and figure out how many you will need to order. Add fifty or more to your final total before you turn in your order. It's safe to say you (and whoever's helping you) will probably make some mistakes addressing the invitations—and, anyway, you might want to save a few as souvenirs of the big day.

Place your order at least three months before the wedding. If you're really pressed for time, ask to get your envelopes in advance so that you can start addressing them while you're waiting for the invitations to be printed.

Make sure you receive a sample of everything before the full order is printed so that you can proofread it beforehand. Check carefully for typos and spelling errors.

Address for success

There are certain guidelines that you may want to follow when it comes to addressing your invitations.

- ❏ Enlist a few good friends or family members with decent handwriting to help you out.
- ❏ Use black ink only.
- ❏ Don't typewrite the envelopes or use premade labels. Write everything out by hand.
- ❏ Make sure that the same person who's writing on the inside of the invitation addresses the outer envelope.

And about those outer envelopes. . .

- ❏ Always address people formally as Mrs., Mr., Ms., or Miss, unless you feel comfortable enough with them to use names only.
- ❏ With the exception of Mr., Mrs., and the like, do not use abbreviations.
- ❏ If you opt for a formal means of address, refer to a married couple as "Mr. and Mrs. Stephen Michael McGill."
- ❏ If you prefer a more casual means of address,

you might refer to a married couple as "Linda and Stephen McGill." Whether you go with formal or casual is up to you. Only you know your friends and family well enough to say which way is best.

❑ For some couples, you may have to use something like this: "Ms. Linda Ann Smith and Mr. Stephen McGill."

❑ If you are inviting the whole family, simply include the phrase "and family" after the parents' names.

And the inner envelopes?

❑ General address can be more casual: "Mr. and Mrs. McGill" or "Linda and Stephen."

❑ For the whole family: "Mr. and Mrs. McGill, Andrea, Paul, and Meg" or "Linda, Stephen, Andrea, Paul, and Meg."

❑ Anyone over the age of eighteen should receive a separate invitation.

❑ Even though the groom's parents already

know the specifics of the wedding, send them an invitation anyway.

Pack 'em up and ship 'em out

Chances are you'll sit down with your invitations, your response cards, your reception cards, and your return envelopes and wonder how the heck you're going to fit all that in one envelope without unsightly lumps. Well, here's how.

❏ Place the response card face-up under the flap of the response card envelope.

❏ Place a small piece of tissue paper over the lettering on the invitation.

❏ Put any extra enclosures (reception cards, maps, directions) inside the invitation.

❏ Put the response card and envelope inside the invitations as well. The lettering should be facing upward.

❏ Place the invitation inside of the inner envelope with the lettering facing the back flap. Don't seal this

envelope.

- [ ] Put the inner envelope inside the outer envelope; again, the writing on the inner envelope should face the flap of the outer envelope.
- [ ] Seal the outer envelope. Make sure the envelope is properly addressed and contains your return address.
- [ ] Stamp and mail.
- [ ] Note: Because of heavy paper and inserts your invitations may require more than standard first-class stamps. A standard first-class stamp will suffice for the return envelope—but remember, you have to provide this stamp as well.

Additional stationery

Your business with the stationery store (or private printer) usually doesn't end with the invitations. You'll probably be needing thank-you notes, which most couples choose to have done professionally—although it's also appropriate to send notes on personal stationery.

Below is a list of other stationery items you might need to order, depending on your situation—and your budget.

- ❏ Printed directions and/or maps
- ❏ Announcements
- ❏ Ceremony cards (if your ceremony is in a public place)
- ❏ Pew cards (to reserve pews for special family members and friends)
- ❏ Rain cards (to notify guests of an alternate location in the event—oh no!—of rain)
- ❏ Ceremony programs
- ❏ At-home cards (to announce your new address)
- ❏ Name cards (to let the world know whether you've taken your new husband's name, kept yours, hyphentated, or whatever)
- ❏ New personal stationery (modified with your name change)

- ☐ Cocktail napkins featuring the names of you and your groom along with your wedding date
- ☐ Matchbooks or boxes
- ☐ Boxes for the groom's cake

NOTES

_____

_____

_____

_____

_____

_____

_____

_____

_____

_____

_____

_____

_____

_____

_____

_____

_____

_____

_____

_____

_____

_____

_____

_____

_____

_____

_____

_____

_____

_____

_____

_____

_____

_____

_____